Blended Families

THE CHANGING FACE OF MODERN FAMILIES

Adoptive Parents

Blended Families

Celebrity Families

Families Living with Mental
& Physical Challenges

First-Generation Immigrant Families

Foster Families

Gay and Lesbian Parents

Grandparents Raising Kids

Growing Up in Religious Communities

Kids Growing Up Without a Home

Multiracial Families

Single Parents

Teen Parents

What Is a Family?

Blended Families

Rae Simons

Mason Crest Publishers, Inc.

MASON CREST PUBLISHERS INC.
370 Reed Road
Broomall, Pennsylvania 19008
(866)MCP-BOOK (toll free)
www.masoncrest.com

First Printing
9 8 7 6 5 4 3 2 1

Library of Congress Cataloging-in-Publication Data

Simons, Rae, 1957–
Blended families / Rae Simons.
p. cm. — (The changing face of modern families)
Includes bibliographical references and index.
ISBN 978-1-4222-1492-3 — ISBN 978-1-4222-1490-9 (series)
1. Stepfamilies—Juvenile literature. 2. Stepfamilies—United States—Juvenile literature. I. Title.
HQ759.92.S56 2010
306.874'7—dc22
2009026373
Produced by Harding House Publishing Service, Inc. www.hardinghousepages.com
Interior Design by MK Bassett-Harvey.
Cover design by Asya Blue www.asyablue.com.
Printed in The United States of America.

Although the families whose stories are told in this book are made up of real people, in some cases their names have been changed to protect their privacy.

Photo Credits

Creative Commons Attribution ShareAlike: all of olive 52, Baird, Mike 51, jakeliefer 57; Dreamstime: Berger, Andi 15, Lewis, Gary 30, Ravenall, Asleigh 37, Smiers, Ramona 33; iStockphoto 54, AzureLaRoux 37, ClaudiaD 42; United States Department of Health and Human Services 45

ontents

Introduction   6

1. Combining Two Families into One   8

2. Being a Stepmom   28

3. Being a Stepdad   41

4. Being a Stepchild   50

Find Out More   60

Bibliography   62

Index   63

About the Author and the Consultant   64

Introduction

The Gallup Poll has become synonymous with accurate statistics on what people really think, how they live, and what they do. Founded in 1935 by statistician Dr. George Gallup, the Gallup Organization continues to provide the world with unbiased research on who we really are.

From recent Gallup Polls, we can learn a great deal about the modern family. For example, a June 2007 Gallup Poll reported that Americans, on average, believe the ideal number of children for a family to have these days is 2.5. This includes 56 percent of Americans who think it is best to have a small family of one, two, or no children, and 34 percent who think it is ideal to have a larger family of three or more children; nine percent have no opinion. Another recent Gallup Poll found that when Americans were asked, "Do you think homosexual couples should or should not have the legal right to adopt a child," 49 percent of Americans said they should, and 48 percent said they shouldn't; 43 percent supported the legalization of gay marriage, while 57 percent did not. Yet another poll found that 34 percent of Americans feel a conflict between the demands of their professional life and their family life; 39 percent still believe that one parent should ideally stay home with the children while the other works.

Keep in mind that Gallup Polls do not tell us what is right or wrong. They don't report on what people should think—only on what they do think. And what is clear from Gallup Polls is that while the shape of families is changing in our modern world, the concept of family is still vital to our sense of who we are and how we interact with others. An indication of this is the 2008 Gallup poll that found that three out of four Americans reported that family values are important, while one in three said they are "extremely" important.

And how do Americans define "family values"? According to the same poll, here's what Americans say is their definition of a family: a strong unit where faith and morals, education and integrity play important roles within the structure of a committed relationship.

The books in the series demonstrate that strong family units come in all shapes and sizes. Those differences, however, do not change the faith, integrity, and commitment of the families who tell their stories within these books.

1 Combining Two Families into One

Remember the stepmother in Cinderella? She was a cruel woman who loved only her own children and had no room in her heart for her husband's daughter. Or what about Hansel and Gretel's stepmother who abandoned them in the woods? Or Snow White's stepmother who plotted her death with a poison apple? Clearly, these "blended families" were complete and utter failures! Thanks to these fairy tales, the words "wicked" and "stepmother" are forever linked together in many children's minds.

At the extreme opposite are TV sitcoms like the old show from the seventies, *The Brady Bunch*, and movies like *Yours, Mine, and Ours,* which portray blended

What Is the Nuclear Family?

"Nuclear family" is a term that's come to be used for the two-parent version of a family. The words imply that the family can function on its own, without help from outsiders. It's a family model that hasn't been around all that long, though, and it doesn't exist in many parts of the world.

Historical records tell us that the nuclear family arrangement is a relatively recent one. Until recently, few families could afford to live independently, and generations and extended families often lived together. After World War II, though, both the United States and Canada experienced a renewed interest in "the home." As people recovered from the destruction and terror of war, they wanted to build a safe world—and the family unit became a symbol of security. Women who had been forced to take jobs in factories while the men were gone to war now returned to more traditional *gender roles*. Most people believed that men should be the primary wage earners and women should spend their time taking care of the home and raising children.

Historians say that the nuclear family owes a lot to the business practices of car manufacturer Henry Ford, such as the "8-hour day, $5 week," and the New Deal policies of President Franklin D. Roosevelt. These enabled more and more families to be economically independent, to own their own home—and to build a little "nucleus" of security within their own families.

9

According to the U.S. Bureau of Census:

- 1300 new stepfamilies are forming every day.
- Over 50% of U.S. families are remarried or re-coupled.
- The average marriage in America lasts only seven years.
- 50% of the 60 million children under the age of 13 are currently living with one biological parent and that parent's current partner.

family life as though it were a nothing but a barrel of laughs. In these make-believe worlds, stepbrothers and stepsisters, stepmothers and stepfathers are all magically and immediately transformed into a single family unit whose only challenge is the sheer number of household members.

The reality is somewhere in the middle. Like all families, blended families face their share of challenges. Some of these are common to every family; some are unique to blended households. But blended households are no longer unusual (in fact, in the United States, blended families now outnumber traditional nuclear families), which means that more and more households are facing these challenges.

The Statistics

Researchers tell us that based on current divorce *trends*, the number of blended families is likely to grow throughout the twenty-first century. In the United States, an estimated 50 percent of first marriages end in divorce after an average of eleven years. Many of the individuals getting divorced have children—and many will remarry.

Going through a divorce is costly. In terms of dollars and cents, it reduces the standards of living of both ex-spouses. It is also costly in terms of emotional stress; psychologists rank divorce as one of the most stressful events a family can encounter—and each year, a million American children experience divorce firsthand.

However, many of these children will not be in single-parent homes for long. That's because 80 percent of divorced men and 75 percent of divorced women remarry within three to four years. And divorced adults with children tend to remarry quicker than divorced adults without children. What this means in the long run is that half of all children born since 1970 will live in a blended family arrangement.

Many fairy tales feature a stepmother who is cruel to her stepchildren. This image depicts Snow White's stepmother, who attempts to have her stepdaughter killed.

The Children in Blended Families: What the Research Says

"Blended families" were once known as "broken families"—and though society is striving to remove the negative overtones, the fact remains that children in blended families have experienced a serious loss. No matter how positive the new family system may be, these children have lost the old reality they once took for granted. The emotional stress may have negative impacts on children's ability to thrive emotionally, as well as intellectually and physically.

Psychologist Judith Wallerstein, author of *The Unexpected Legacy of Divorce: A 25-Year Landmark Study,* followed the lives of ninety-three now-adult children for twenty-five years. In her book, she reports that 41 percent of these individuals were "doing poorly, worried, *underachieving*, *deprecating*, and often angry." According to Wallerstein, most of the individuals felt they lacked a "working model for a loving relationship between a man and a woman." She also found that many parents in blended homes "are unable to separate their needs from the children's needs and often share too much of their personal life with their children, placing the children in a *precarious* emotional state, *vulnerable* to *grandiosity* or to depression within what is left of their families."

But Wallerstein's report isn't all bad news. She found that after a divorce, children tend to do well if their mothers and fathers take up their parenting roles once more, put their differences aside, and allow the children to continue to have relationships with both parents, regardless of remarriage.

E. Mavis Hetherington, another psychologist who studied 1,400 families over thirty years, also found that blended families have both negative and positive qualities. According to Hetherington:

- Most children are doing reasonably well within two years of the divorce.
- About 25 percent of children from divorced families have serious social or emotional problems, while only 10 percent from intact families do.
- Most young adults who grew up in blended families, however, are establishing careers, creating intimate relationships, and building meaningful lives.
- Young women in blended families do better than young men, often becoming more *competent* than if they had stayed in unhappy family situations.

Elizabeth Marquardt, another researcher, surveyed 1,500 young adults between the ages of 18 and 35, half of whom were from blended families and half from intact families. She found that the most difficult challenge for children in blended households is going back and forth between two homes and two families, especially when these households are very different from

each other in terms of values and expectations. Judith Wallerstein agrees. "These children have a sense of living in two different worlds," she writes. "They grow up with a difficulty in feeling whole."

Other Challenges to Blended Families

You might think that blended families recover from their earlier challenges and go on to live happily ever

What Is a Family?

The U.S. Census Bureau defines a family as "two or more people, one of whom is the householder, related by birth, marriage, or adoption and residing in the same housing unit. A household consists of all people who occupy a housing unit regardless of relationship. A household may consist of a person living alone or multiple unrelated individuals or families living together."

According to the United Nations, "The family is the natural and fundamental group unit of society and is entitled to protection by society and the State"

The National Institute of Mental Health wanted to address the family's changing reality over the past few decades and came up with this definition: "A family is a network of mutual commitment."

The television show The Brady Bunch created an idyllic view of life in a blended family. In reality, there are many challenges facing a blended family, and not all survive.

after. Unfortunately, that's not always the case: more than 60 percent of blended families are re-broken because of yet another divorce. This is stressful for everyone concerned, but especially for the children who are involved.

Experts list several reasons for blended families' failures. These include the couple not being prepared for:

• disputes over parenting
• feelings of favoritism for birth children
• jealousy and hostility between step-siblings

- stress over visitation schedules, especially around the holidays
- rejection of stepparents by stepchildren

All these are perfectly normal tensions, but if the family is not prepared for them, family members may feel guilty and overwhelmed.

Blending two families into one family is not easy—but it is possible. Counselors say it is important that blended families follow specific patterns for success:

- Acknowledge and mourn the loss of the original family, including the hopes and dreams for it that never came to be. Allow children to express their feelings in settings where they can be honest without worrying about hurting or offending anyone.
- Have realistic expectations. It takes time to become family, and it takes time to learn to love one another. Don't worry if stepchildren don't instantly love each other and their stepparents. Experts say it can take four to seven years before a blended family truly views itself as a unit.
- As stepparents, put your marriage first. Make your relationship a priority, and be loyal to one another.
- Don't try to replace birth parents with stepparents. Allow children to form whatever relationship makes them most comfortable with their step-

parent. Don't force children to call stepparents "Mom" or "Dad." Allow biological parents to handle discipline for the first year or so.

• Develop new traditions and rituals that are unique to the new blended family and that will work around visitation schedules. Be flexible enough to let go of traditions that don't work well with the blended family's demands.

• Get support, whether from a faith-based group, a counselor, or a support group. Find a safe place to share challenges and seek advice.

For children, the challenges of a blended family are especially difficult. Blended families are usually formed because of a loss, and nobody in the family experiences that loss more than the children. Kids have lost control and continuity in their life. They have had no choice in the parent's decisions, yet their lives have been changed forever. Most likely, children have lost daily contact with one parent. They may also have moved, changing schools and leaving behind neighborhood friends and their home. If this has happened, they've in effect lost everything that was familiar and safe. Remarriage of one or both parents may also threaten the close bonds that often develop between child and parent in a single-parent family—and learning to share a parent with another adult may create additional feelings of loss for children. Children in blended families may feel like they

Experts say that blended families tend to go through seven stages:

1. **Fantasy Stage**: Most people bring fantasies, wishes, and unspoken expectations to their new relationships.
2. **Immersion Stage**: The reality of blending a family begins to be felt; the stepparent has an outsider position and biological parent and child remain intensely connected.
3. **Awareness Stage**: Fantasies of an instant family are let go and the stepparent begins to know the strangers he or she has joined. Biological parents begin to understand more clearly that they are the only ones truly connected to both children and spouse.
4. **Mobilization Stage**: Differences are much more openly expressed; this may be a *chaotic*, stressful period. Stepparents may begin speaking up with more energy about their needs for *inclusion* and for change.
5. **Action Stage**: This is the stage where *negotiations* are made about how the family will function. Moves in this stage change the family structure as new boundaries are drawn. The family now has enough understanding so that every family activity is no longer a potential power struggle between insiders and outsiders. Moving to this stage too quickly can cause major problems and stress.

6. **Contact Stage**: There is less attention to step issues and this is often the honeymoon stage. It is only now that a clearly defined stepparent role begins to emerge.
7. **Resolution Stage**: The stepfamily now has solid and reliable relationships; Although some children may be more inside the family than others, there is clarity about and acceptance of this fact; The stepparent role now brings satisfaction and nourishment.

Movement through the stages does not happen neatly and precisely. A family may move ahead in one area but remain at a much earlier stage in another. According to experts, some families complete the entire cycle in about four years, but most families take about seven years. Many of the families end in divorce, others remain stuck, but some will eventually move on successfully. These families usually have fewer deeply held fantasies and more realistic expectations.

(Adapted from Winning Stepfamilies, www.winningstepfamilies. com.)

are forever in transition as they move between the homes of their biological parents. These children may have to cope with having friends and possessions in two different places, along with two sets of routines and rules.

As blended families become more and more common, however, these challenges will no longer seem so unusual, and more support will be offered to these families. Instant family unity and harmony is not a reality for blended families any more than it is for any other family. When people live together in the same household, there are bound to be tensions to work out, regardless of whether they are connected biologically or not.

The families who shared their stories for this book have learned that being a family means facing those tensions and learning to work past them. The bonds they've formed (or that are still forming) didn't come automatically. Instead, they grew from the shared challenge of living together. Each of these blended families are a group of people who are committed to living together and taking care of each other—and ultimately, that's what a family really is.

What Do You Think?

What is your definition of the word "family"? In your opinion, what is the most important requirement for being a family?

HEADLINES

(From "Making Blended Families Work" by Kimberly Davis, *Ebony*, October 2000."

When Kerry and Deborah Henry of Feyetteville, N.C., married two years ago, the couple, along with his two teenagers and her young son, became one of the more than 1,300 stepfamilies formed in America every day.

Although they dated for three years before they married, they knew that blending their families wouldn't be easy. "The odds are always against blended families. I knew it wasn't going to be like *The Brady Bunch*," says the newlywed husband, a cellular network engineer. "That's TV."

Their new, blended family included Kerry's daughter, Danielle, now 14, and son, Da-Shaun, 18, who's in the U.S. Army, as well as Deborah's 9-year-old son, Curtis Thompson. All three children had been used to the way things were, but that didn't stop the couple from making a commitment to each other and to making their lives together work.

"Our first priority was us," says Deborah Henry, a hairstylist. "We wanted to be a family."

Before marrying, the couple conferred with their children, who gave their stamp of approval and later

joined the wedding party. And not only did the new family start fresh in a new home, each child had his or her own room.

"I asked their permission, and they told me that they wanted to see me happy," the new husband says of his two children. "I was content with putting my personal happiness after theirs. They made me realize that they could be happy and that I could be happy, too."

Experts say this is the way to blend a family. For stepfamilies to work, the married couple has to show loving, patient and tolerant behavior. They also have to recognize the rights and feelings of their children and stepchildren. No matter how long their preparation, however, there will probably be a period of adjustment. Blended families have the same challenges and struggles as any traditional families.

The challenges include dealing with the feelings, thoughts and emotions of the children and stepchildren. Children sometimes feel that they are betraying their biological parent by forming a new and loving relationship with a stepparent. They may also try to shoulder the blame for the failure of their natural parents' marriage.

"No matter how good the relationship is between the biological parents [after the separation]," says Dr. S. Malone-Hawkins, a sociologist at Texas Woman's

University in Denton, Texas, "there are going to be those instances when children feel guilty about the failure of [their biological parents'] relationship."

That's where the parents and the extended family must step in to make sure the children understand that they are loved and that the failure of their biological parents' marriage is not their fault. An effective strategy for doing this is to maintain a good relationship with the biological parent and to demonstrate good behavior for the extended family, including grandparents, aunts, uncles and cousins.

"People need to be grown-up about these things," says Dr. Malone-Hawkins, herself a stepchild and a stepmother. "They need to be models for the children."

And although some might expect the relationship to be *adversarial*, Henry says he and Curtis' father have become close.

"I did not want him to lose sight of the fact that he has a father," the new stepfather says of Curtis and his biological father. "We get along very well. It's strange; we're very good friends."

Most of all, stepfamilies have to realize that it will take time to open up, share feelings and become a family. It is important to establish a permanent rela-

tionship, hopefully even a friendship, with your step-children, says Deborah, who exchanges letters with her stepson, Da-Shaun. He now calls her his second mother, the ultimate *tribute* any stepparent can have. With Danielle, who formerly was the woman of the house, the situation is a bit more difficult. But they're on the way.

"As time goes on and they see that I'm not going anywhere, they'll probably open up more," says Deborah, who won her stepchildren over with her cooking. "It's not something that you rush."

Jackie Wimbush of Clinton, Md., faced an entirely different set of circumstances when he became a stepfather. Ten years ago, Wimbush married his wife, Rolita, when her son Ryland was just a toddling 2-year-old. The school bus driver and minister says he made a choice to become Ryland's father, and it was a difficult decision to make at first. That's only natural, experts say, because accepting responsibility for someone else's child is a large step that shouldn't be taken lightly.

"I was wondering whether I wanted to pursue a marriage with these types of issues," Wimbush says. "That was the challenge for me."

Then he decided that it would be "an honor" to be Ryland's father, and that it would be worth it to fight for his relationship with Rolita, with whom he now has an 8-year-old son, Jackie II. "I love this lady," Wimbush remembers saying to himself. "I'm not going to allow my stuff to get in the way."

What Do You Think?

In terms of the stages blended families go through, outlined earlier in this chapter, where do you think each of the families described in this article are at? Do you think they will succeed at blending their families together successfully? What are they doing right? Do you think they are doing anything wrong?

HEADLINES

(From "Researcher Finds Correlation Between Blended Families and Grades" by Patty Harrison, WCTV, April 23, 2008, www.wctv.tv/home/headlines/18149244.html.)

When we think of blended families, we think of the "Brady Bunch."

But if the 70s favorite became reality, researcher Kathryn Tillman says the group that "somehow formed a family" would be dealing with a lot more than sitcom squabbles.

Kathryn Tillman is an Assistant Professor at Florida State University and her research has just hit big—as it's been published in the journal *Social Science Research*.

But it's not just the study's publishing that's gaining interest, it's its findings too.

Tillman says adolescents living in blended families—with half or step siblings—have lower grades and more school related behavior problems than their peers.

"You get the situation where kids may feel more conflict, they may feel more in competition with each other. Parents are all of a sudden having to shift attention and shift resources between children and that can be difficult for kids to adapt to," said Tillman.

School guidance counselors agree with Tillman's research.

However they say, with the proper *precautions*, parents can deal with major family structure changes by being honest with their children.

They recommend notifying your child's school if you expect any drastic changes in family structure.

"Children often feel when there's something of a crisis nature going on in their family that they are the only ones who ever have experienced it before and sometimes we'll have a group just so the kids can see that other kids are grappling with the same kind of problems they are," said guidance counselor Diane Scheiner.

According to the study, it's the boys living in blended families that appear to have the hardest time coping.

They're reported to having average GPA's one quarter of a letter grade lower than those who only live with full siblings.

What Do You Think?

According to this article, why should we pay attention to what Kathryn Tillman says about blended families? Do you respect Tillman's findings? Why or why not? Why do you think boys have a harder time living in blended families than girls do? How do you think blended families should help their children cope better with school demands?

2 Being a Stepmom

Terms to Understand

contention: disagreement, argument, controversy.
consensus: general agreement.
caveat: warning, qualification.

When Regina met Tom, she had no wish to have children, or even to get married. Tom, however, already had a six-month-old son named Andrew, and three older daughters by previous marriages. He didn't really see the girls much, but he wanted a relationship with Andrew.

As Regina fell in love with Tom, she wondered about becoming a stepmother and what her life would hold. Her mother, too, was concerned, wanting the best for Regina, but when she saw that Regina truly loved Tom, she was supportive.

Not long after Regina and Tom married, their own daughter, Jade, was born. The original plan was to have eighteen-month-old Andrew live with them as well, but after Tom lost his job, things didn't work out as they had hoped. Andrew's mother continued to have custody of him.

For the next several years, Andrew visited Regina and Tom every other weekend and for a week or more each summer. His life at home with his mother was

Child Custody

When a married couple gets divorced, they must agree on who gets custody of the children. "Custody" can mean a couple of things: the legal authority to make decisions affecting a child's interests (legal custody) and the responsibility of taking care of the child (physical custody). When parents separate or divorce, one of the hardest decisions they have to make is which parent will have custody. The most common arrangement is for one parent to have custody (both physical and legal) while the other parent has a right of visitation. But it is not uncommon for the parents to share legal custody, even though one parent has physical custody.

If parents cannot agree on who has custody, the court system will make the decision for them. "The best interest of the child" is the deciding factor courts use when awarding custody. Some states hold that the best interest of the child is to have frequent contact with both parents; in this case, the parent who is most supportive of this arrangement is more likely to be the custodian. Factors such as a proposed move or undermining the other parent will be taken very seriously by the court. Ultimately, however, the best interests of the child will vary from situation to situation.

often unstable, and Andrew often didn't know whether he would be sleeping at home or at his grandparents' house, where his mother frequently left him.

The summer that Andrew turned eight, his mother arranged with Regina and Tom for him to go live with them. He would go on vacation and then move in right before school started in the fall. Andrew and Jade, who were close friends, were both excited about the idea. Regina and Tom got things ready for Andrew's arrival. They registered him in school and set up his room.

When parents get divorced, children can feel hurt, stressed and angry. Parents need to provide emotional support to the child, and protect him from feeling caught in the middle.

Then, just before he was to move in, Andrew's mother called and said she'd changed her mind.

Jade was angry, and Andrew was devastated. He began to have problems in school, falling behind in his work and getting into trouble. When he was with Regina and Tom he had stability and a routine that life with his mother was lacking, and he often felt unsettled and uneasy. Regina and Tom met with his teachers to see what they could do to help, but it was difficult when he was away from them so often.

The next June, around the time Andrew turned nine, his mother agreed to have him move in with Regina and Tom. She acknowledged that her lifestyle made it difficult to give him any kind of stability.

Since then, a year ago, Andrew has lived with Regina, Tom, and Jade, visiting his mother and grandparents every other weekend and for vacations. He and Jade are best friends, and he's doing better in school as well.

When Regina thinks back to her concerns before she married Tom, wondering what it would be like to be a stepmother, she's happy with the way things have turned out. "If it wasn't for Andrew," Regina says, "Jade would be an only child."

Despite the fact that she and Andrew were so close, Jade did have some adjustment issues when he first came to live with them. She was used to having her parents all to herself most of the time. She was jealous of the attention Regina and Tom gave to Andrew.

Her moods were stormy and her behavior difficult for a while, but gradually, the family adjusted to the extra member.

"Andrew's a great kid," Regina says. "He has problems, but he has a great sense of humor. He's very loving. He does need more attention because of how he grew up, because he felt like he didn't have a home. He was always staying with various people—his mom, his grandparents, others. Now he has a more stable life. He knows what to expect.

"Kids in blended families are lucky in some ways," Regina adds. "They have a larger family and support group. It can be harder for Jade because she doesn't have that. She's jealous sometimes of what her brother has that she doesn't."

And that's one of the biggest challenges Regina and her family face. Because Andrew has a whole other family that Jade doesn't, she sometimes feels left out when he does things with them. He goes on vacations with his grandparents in the summer and comes home chattering about the places they have gone and the fun things they've done. Meanwhile, Jade hasn't had any of those experiences; it doesn't seem fair to her.

On the other hand, if Regina and Tom do something special with Jade while Andrew is away, Andrew feels left out. Both Jade and Andrew feel as though somehow time should stop for the other while they are apart.

Stepsiblings can form a close bond like any other siblings. Unlike biological siblings, they have to learn that having two families means missing out on some parts of each other's lives.

For Regina and Tom, the challenge is often scheduling with Andrew's mother or grandparents. They might plan something, for example, only to have Andrew's mother call and ask to have him that weekend for something special she had planned. Planning ahead and managing time with the other family has been an ongoing learning process for Regina and Tom.

Regina feels she has been very fortunate in her marriage to Tom. Not only is she a mother to both Jade and Andrew, but she has also been able to form relationships with Tom's two oldest daughters, who live in another part of the country. "I have two step-daughters

This chart shows the percentages of children under the age of 18 in different two parent living situations. A total of 22% of the children surveyed live in some form of blended family.

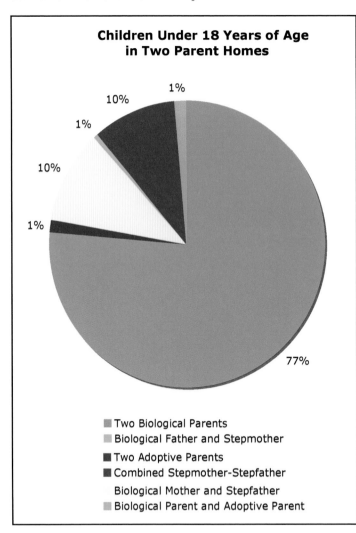

Children Under 18 Years of Age in Two Parent Homes

1%
10%
1%
10%
1%
77%

■ Two Biological Parents
▨ Biological Father and Stepmother
■ Two Adoptive Parents
■ Combined Stepmother-Stepfather
  Biological Mother and Stepfather
▨ Biological Parent and Adoptive Parent

who are grown women," she says. "They accepted me and made me part of their lives."

She thinks as well that becoming Andrew's step-mother has helped her marriage with Tom. His second marriage had been destroyed after his wife had refused to accept Tom's daughter. "Tom appreciates that I treat Andrew like he's my child," she says. "But it's not hard, because that's how I feel about him."

What Do You Think?

When you look back at the strategies listed in chapter 1 for building a successful blended family, which ones do you think Regina and her family have achieved? Where do you think they are at in the stages listed on pages 18–19?

HEADLINES

(From "How We Manage Our Blended Family" by Erika Rasmusson Janes, *Redbook*, www.redbookmag.com/kids-family/advice/blended-family-hl.)

For Melissa and Chris Ellsworth, a trip to Burger King brings back memories of when their romance was first brewing three years ago. "We met and immediately went to having dates at Burger King with four kids!"

says Melissa, 31, who, like Chris, has two children from her previous marriage. "We would go there and leave the kids in the playroom so we could talk."

These days, though, Melissa and Chris, 33, who were married in 2004, are more likely to grab dinner for six from the drive-through window and rush home to the kids (Andrew, 6, and Emily, 4, from Chris's first marriage, and Anthony, 12, and Taryn, 5, from Melissa's) than sit down and chat. And working to-gether—Melissa owns a home inspection company that Chris works for—ups their stress, but not their quality time. Both admit that the challenge of mesh-ing their two families has been tough: Rather than enjoying their new partnership, they find themselves arguing about how to discipline the kids, and how to deal with their exes and their exes' families. "Our life is more about what's going on with the kids, not us," says Chris. "It feels like we're taking each other for granted sometimes."

Melissa and Chris are facing issues that naturally come up in all blended families, says Norman Epstein, Ph.D., a . . . professor of family studies at the Univer-sity of Maryland, and a licensed marital and family therapist. "If Chris and Melissa continue to neglect their marriage in order to meet the children's needs, it'll leave them feeling lonely and isolated from each other, and that's bad for them and their kids," he says. Once Melissa and Chris feel closer as a couple, it'll be easier for them to tackle raising the children and dealing with each other's families.

An especially touchy issue for Melissa and Chris is how to discipline each other's kids. "We're trying to be a unified front, but we still let the other have the final say on what our own kids do," says Melissa. "We don't communicate as well as we should about it either—we sort of tiptoe around the issue."

Parents of a bended family may find themselves clashing over the proper care of the children. Difficulties during transition are normal—couples should work out a way to combine parenting styles over time.

The relationship between a stepmother and her stepchild will not always be easy, but it can be loving and rewarding.

Where and how the kids sleep is also a point of *contention*. "We've argued over it," says Melissa, explaining that Chris and his ex used to allow Emily to sleep with them, but she wants to break that habit. Chris is on board, but has found it hard to follow through. "I have to lie down with Emily every night in order for her to fall asleep," he says. And as soon as Emily seems to be getting used to sleeping in her own room,

it's time for the custody swap (Chris and his ex-wife each have custody of their kids every other week)—and any progress is undone, since Emily sleeps with her mother.

The expert's advice: Think and act like a team.

Because they each have their own way of parenting, it's crucial that Chris and Melissa sit down and discuss what they want when it comes to sleep arrangements, and other family issues, and as much as possible come to a *consensus*. "Every time Melissa and Chris reach a middle ground, they'll see that their preferences are respected and taken into account, which will make them feel closer as a couple," says Epstein. One *caveat*: When it comes to discipline, it's actually not a bad idea for Chris to be the authority with his own kids and Melissa with hers. It's even okay if they each set different rules—at least initially, says Epstein. If the kids are forced to follow the same rules and be disciplined by their stepparent, they may feel pushed into accepting the stepparent as their own mom or dad, which is likely to interrupt the bonding process. Still, "each parent has to be consistent with his or her own rules and express respect and support for the other's way of doing things," says Epstein. As everyone gets more used to one another, Chris and Melissa can mesh their strategies little by little.

What Do You Think?

How is the family of Chris and Melissa like any family? How is it different? How good of a job do you think Chris and Melissa are doing at facing the challenges of being a blended family?

3 Being a Stepdad

When Harry met his new neighbor Amy, it was love at first sight. The next week, he met Amy's sister Lisa, and he fell in love all over again. Amy was three and Lisa was four, and when he finally met their mom, Denise, he felt like he'd come home. By the end of the month, he was sure he wanted to spend the rest of his life with Denise and her two little girls.

Terms to Understand

preconceptions: opinions or ideas formed before evidence or knowledge is gained.

Denise took a little longer to convince. She'd gone through a painful divorce not that long ago, and she wasn't ready to risk being involved with another man yet. Her children were the most important thing in her life, and she didn't even want to date Harry, for fear the girls would get attached to him and then end up hurt if things didn't work out between them.

But Harry never had any doubts. "I just hung in there with Denise and was patient. And in the meantime, I went to the playground with the girls. I helped out around the house whenever I could. I did my best

A single mother with young children may avoid dating. Any man she dates is also involved with her children, who can be hurt if the relationship doesn't last.

to prove to Denise that I wasn't going anywhere, that I was someone she could trust."

Eventually, Denise was convinced, and she and Harry were married. Amy and Lisa were flower girls. They told everyone about the wedding. "'We married Harry,' they'd say, and I felt so good that they loved me," Harry recalls. "We settled into being a family as though we'd been one all along."

But two years later, when Amy was six and Lisa was seven, the family's life faced a new complication: Harry's twelve-year-old son joined the household. Suddenly, everything changed.

For most of his life, Derek had lived with his mother on the other side of the country. Harry and Derek's mother had divorced when he was a baby, and Harry had only seen his son a handful of times since then. Now Derek's mom was seriously ill, and she needed to send Derek to stay with Harry while she went through treatment.

"Derek was scared and confused and mad at the world," Harry remembers. "His whole life, everything he'd always known, had disappeared on him. He didn't trust me, and he didn't know what to think of Denise and the girls. And on their side, they didn't know what to think of him. Denise wanted to love him, but he just wasn't all that loveable right at this moment of his life. He was a big, heavy kid who scowled all the time. The

girls were shy around him, and he didn't know how to act around them. It was all really hard."

To make matters even worse, Harry and Denise began fighting over the kids' discipline. "I couldn't help but be protective of Derek," Harry explains. "I could see how he felt, and I wanted to give him a break. But Denise was protective of the girls. She worried about them for fear Derek might do something inappropriate around them, something that would damage them in some way. That made me angry, that she could think that about Derek. For the first time ever in our relationship, we fought all the time."

Harry and Denise tried to hide their disagreements from the children. "But they couldn't help but feel the tension in the air. And then all three of them acted worse than they would have otherwise. They bickered with each other all the time. It got on my nerves and on Denise's, and then we took it out on each other."

The turning point came after Derek had been with them about six months. "We were driving along in the car," Harry says, "and all five of us were arguing. And then Lisa said, 'You know what we sound like? We sound like a family.' Denise and I looked at each other, and then we started laughing. The kids didn't get what we thought was so funny. But it was like all of a sudden, both Denise and I had hope."

Harry and Denise decided to go to family counseling. "We figured we were already a family—we just needed

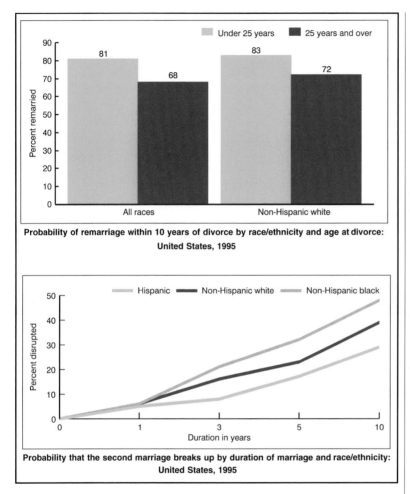

Probability of remarriage within 10 years of divorce by race/ethnicity and age at divorce: United States, 1995

Probability that the second marriage breaks up by duration of marriage and race/ethnicity: United States, 1995

As this chart from the U.S. Department of Health and Human Services shows, remarriage within 10 years of divorce is quite common. Unfortunately, the probability that a second marriage will break up within 10 years is quite high. Seeing a marriage or family counselor may help increase a blended family's chances of survival.

some help learning how to get along, the way all families do sometimes."

The counselor worked with all five members of the family, both individually and as a group. "It wasn't like all our problems went away magically," Harry says. "Denise and I still argued over the kids. She still accused me of loving Derek more than the girls, and

I still accused her of not being fair to Derek. But the counselor gave us better ways to fight, ways that didn't hurt us so much. Now we weren't fighting so much as sharing our feelings, and we learned to say thing in ways that helped us understand each other better. Denise and I started spending more time together, without any of the kids. The counselor said that building our own relationship and making it strong was the most important thing we could do for the kids."

When the time came for Derek to go home to his mom, the entire family was sad to see him go—but they were glad he would be back for Christmas and summer vacations. "We really are a family now," Harry says. "No family is perfect, and neither is ours. But we love each other, and that's what really matters."

What Do You Think?

What did Harry and Denise do right in their blended family? What did they do wrong?
Describe this same story from Derek's perspective.
How do you think his story will be different from Harry's?
What about the same story from
Lisa or Amy's point of view?

HEADLINES

(From "One Stepfather's Advice" by Paul Thurman, ezinearticles. com/?One-Stepfathers-Advice&id=2136122.)

Six years ago I divorced my first wife, moved to the UK, and married my second wife. At the time her sons were three and four. After only a short time I loved them as my own. In fact I allowed a part of me to believe that's is what they were. I began to chase this fantastical belief with great passion and focus spurred on by my wife's approval and their acceptance. It seemed so perfect. My dreams and plans continued to soar year after year. Then one day, three years after my arrival, I became brave enough to share my thoughts and feelings with the boys. I even told them that I'd be honoured if they'd call me Dad. My heart was filled with pride and joy when they initially embraced the idea (in fact one even literally cheered).

Two days later I was gutted! When the boys returned from a visit with their paternal father wound up and distraught over a conversation they had with him. After speaking with him, both felt that I'd made a force play and put them in a position that I had no right to. What could I do but watch all my *preconceptions* burst into flames and wonder about what role I'd have in the lives of the boys. I felt furious at their father for causing them to rise against me. I blamed him for stealing them from me for months.

Looking back at this scenario years later I can still feel the desolation I felt back then, but I can also look back with more understanding and wisdom. I didn't realise it at the time, but I was really being selfish. I convinced myself I was doing the best thing for the boys when in reality it would've been the best thing for me. You see, when I divorced my first wife, she went against everything we agreed on and took full custody of my three children. So, when I arrived in the UK I arrived with a huge hole in my heart. I missed my children so very much and I saw the potential of the boys filling that void. Without thinking about it, I'd foisted my need off onto the boys and persuaded myself I was doing them a service. And I stayed in that fantasy for three years until that fateful day when they set me straight.

Walking into a family and becoming a stepfather is a huge task. It must be done with a great amount of humility and the understanding that you're there as an extension to the children's family rather than a replacement (except in cases where the paternal father has done a runner of course). And believe me, it never ceases to be a balancing act. A stepfather must support the healthy growth of his children whilst being oh so careful not to undermine what they have going with their paternal father. Sometimes I feel like I spend more time trying to make things balance out than developing a deep relationship with the boys. Though this may or may not genuinely be the case, the bottom line is that's what the boys need in order to function and grow so that's what I'll do for as long as they need it. Though I'll always be a bit jealous of the stepfathers that get the title of "Dad" from the willing hearts of their stepchildren, I have finally found a peace with just being "Paul" to mine.

To any of you men who read this who are either stepfathers or about to become so, please consider this advice. Take the entire process slow and before you attempt to make any moves forward in your relationships with your stepchildren search your heart and ask yourself, "Is this move forward the very best for the children?" If you get the slightest niggles it might not be, then stop. If you truly love your stepchildren make sure you're putting their needs and not your own first.

What Do You Think?

Do you think the author of this article is a good stepfather? Why or why not? What has he learned that has made him a better father? Do you admire him? Why or why not?

4 Being a Stepchild

Reeva Longstreet is twenty years old, a successful college student with an exciting career mapped out for herself. She's close to her mom, she has plenty of friends who think she's the easiest person in the world to get along with, and she's one of those people who would rather laugh than argue. But Reeva hates her stepfather.

"I mean it," she admits. "I really hate the guy. I can barely stand to be in the same room with him."

Reeva's mom and dad separated before Reeva was even born, so she was never close to her father. While she was growing up, her mom was her best friend; the two of them did everything together, went everywhere together, talked about everything. "Maybe she spoiled me," Reeva says, "but it didn't seem like that to me at the time. She and I would stay up late on the weekends watching movies together and eating brownies. We went on trips together, we went shopping together. I couldn't wait to come home from school so I could tell her about my

Terms to Understand

empathy: identifying with and understanding another's situation, emotions, etc.

A single mother and her only daughter can share a special bond that is closer to friendship than a normal parent-child relationship. A daughter who is this close to her mother is liable to feel abandoned if her mother enters into a serious dating relationship.

day. She was more fun than anyone else I knew. And when I was with her, I always felt like I was the most special person in the world."

Over the years, Reeva's mom dated from time to time, but until Reeva was fourteen, there was never anyone serious in her mother's life. "But once she met Dick, everything changed. He was our landlord is how she met him, and he was a lot older than her. I mean a lot, like his mid-fifties when she was only in her late thirties. I just couldn't see what she saw in him. He was always saying these stupid things he thought were funny. When I didn't laugh at his jokes, he acted like I was being rude."

Allowing the children to be involved in the wedding can help make everyone feel like a part of the family. Some blended families even take family vows to promise to love each other and to help strengthen their family bonds.

Reeva's mother dated Dick for more than a year. "She kept asking me permission to get engaged, but I refused to give it to her. I was so angry with her for bringing this guy in our lives. We'd been doing fine before he came along and changed everything. But then my mom's friend talked to me and told me I was being selfish. She said my mom deserved to be happy, that she'd worked so hard as a single mom, and that Dick made her happier than she'd ever seen her before. She said that even if I didn't like Dick, I needed to see how good he was for my mom."

Reeva hated to admit it, but she knew her mother's friend was right. Reluctantly, she gave her mother permission to get married.

Dick had two teenage children of his own, Randy and Yvonne, who were seventeen and eighteen. After the marriage, the families moved into a new home together.

Reeva still missed the days when she had her mother all to herself, but she came to realize that being a blended family had its advantages too. "I hated Dick, but I loved having a big brother and a big sister," Reeva says. "They were enough older than me that I looked up to them. I had a really, really bad case of hero worship. They were cool, though, and really patient with me. Yvonne especially has taught me a lot. And they adore my mom, too. I really think of them as my brother and sister now. We're close. I can't imagine how I got along without them."

But Reeva still doesn't like her stepfather. "I accept him now. I try not to get in fights with him anymore, the way I did when I was younger. For my mom's sake, I try not to let him know how I feel about him. Maybe inside, I'm still just a selfish immature brat. But I can't help it.

Even if a child is generally happy with her new blended family, she may never learn to fully accept her stepparent.

I resent the guy. I don't understand why my mom loves him. He'll never seem like my father."

What would Reeva tell other stepchildren? "I guess try to see things from other people's perspectives. Be realistic in your expectations of the other people in

your family. They're just human beings, with faults and strengths like anyone. Find someone you trust to share your feelings with honestly—a friend or a counselor or someone like that—but don't expect your biological parent to be the one who listens to your feelings. It's okay to be angry and hurt and confused—but it's expecting too much of your biological parent to handle those feelings when they're directed at the person they've fallen in love with. Be patient. If you give yourself and your family time, eventually, maybe you'll build family bonds despite how you feel now." She laughs. "Who knows? Maybe one day, I'll even be able to say I love Dick. But not yet."

What Do You Think?

Why do you think Reeva has head such a hard time accepting her stepfather? Why was she able to accept her stepbrother and stepsister, but not Dick? How do you think Reeva's mom feels? What about Dick? Do you think Reeva is handling the situation as best she can— or is there something she should be doing differently?

HEADLINES

(From "Creating Shared Memories for Your Blended Family: One Family's Experience," Advice for Parents, Cincinnati Children's, www.cincinnatichildrens.org/health/yh/archives/2005/spring/blended-family.htm)

Jean Robson acknowledges that the success of her family is due to all seven members, but she is also "very proud of how it's turned out." She says, "We're so close today that there's nothing that could separate us."

For Jean and Cliff Robson, their traditions have played an important role in bringing their families closer together and in helping both of their individual families become one.

Jean and Cliff met through their church and children's school in 1992. Both were divorced, single parents with second-grade girls at St. Mary's grade school. He also had a son. "I would see Cliff at church with his kids and was impressed," Jean says.

Cliff was impressed also, and the two started dating. After a year they got engaged and bought a house. Six months later the families moved in together, after the wedding.

Cliff introduced his kids, Jacalu and Cliff, then 10 and 8, to the idea of Jean and Tori joining their family by showing them the new house. "I said, 'We're going to move in here,' and they started jumping around." When he added that he and Jean were getting married, the kids were even more excited.

"As he tells it," Jean says, "the kids started doing cartwheels. So I told Tori in the same way, showing her the new house and telling her of the engagement. She burst into tears."

But Tori, just 10 at the time, wasn't crying about having new siblings or her mom getting married. She

Continuing past traditions, like Thanksgiving, can be a challenge for blended families, who have many schedules to consider. Building and sharing new and unique traditions is an important part of making a blended family into just a family.

was upset about not having her own room, a fear quickly put at ease.

"The kids were very involved in the wedding," Jean says. All three kids were in the wedding and after Jean and Cliff said their vows, the whole family took family vows that they had written, promising to love each other.

That vow of love is something Jean and Cliff work on very hard. As a couple, Cliff and Jean always reassure their kids that, "We are now a couple. We have a lot of love for each other and nothing is going to separate us." Jean says, "Our kids have to believe we love each other and love them."

"I have so much *empathy* for people trying to blend families," Jean says. But for her and Cliff, their kids made the meld easy. They also were excited about the idea of getting even more new siblings.

Soon after Jean and Cliff married, they got pregnant with son Will, and a few years later had another son, Charlie.

Blended families have unique challenges. For instance, common traditions, like getting the family together for Thanksgiving dinner, can be hard to manage with varying schedules and multiple parents. "As a new, blended family you can set up your own traditions; these are the memories you create," Jean says.

What Do You Think?

Do you think it was a good idea to have the children say vows to each other at Jean and Cliff's wedding? Why or why not?
Of all the families described in this book, both in the interviews and in the headline articles, which ones do you think are the most successful at being blended families?
What do all these families have in common?
Which ones do you think will continue to have serious problems? Why?

Find Out More

BOOKS

Block, Joel D. and Susan Bartell. *Stepliving for Teens: Getting Along with Stepparents, Parents, and Siblings.* New York: Price Sloan Stern, 2001.

Chedekel, David S. and Karen O'Connell. *The Blended Family Sourcebook: A Guide to Negotiating Change.* New York: McGraw-Hill, 2002.

Cohn, Lisa and Debbie Glasser. *The Step-Tween Survival Guide: How to Deal with Life in a Stepfamily.* Minneapolis: Free Spirit Publishing, 2008.

Copeland, Cynthia L. *The 312 Best Things About Being a Step-mom.* New York: Workman Publishing Company, 2006.

Gillespie, Natalie Nichols. *Stepfamily Success: Practical Solutions for Common Challenges.* Grand Rapids, Mich.: Revell, 2007.

LeBey, Barbara. *Remarried with Children: Ten Secrets for Success-fully Blending and Extending Your Family.* New York: Bantam Dell, 2005.

Lofas, Jannette. *Stepparenting: Everything You Need to Know to Make it Work.* Revised and Updated. New York: Kensington Publishing, 2004.

Marsolini, Maxine. *Raising Children in Blended Families: Helpful Insights, Expert Opinions, and True Stories.* Grand Rapids, Mich.: Kregel, 2006.

Wisdom, Susan and Jennifer Green. *Stepcoupling: Creating and Sustaining a Strong Marriage in Today's Blended Family.* New York: Three Rivers Press, 2002.

Ziegahn, Suzen J. *The Stepparent's Survival Guide: A Workbook for Creating a Happy Blended Family.* Oakland, Calif.: New Harbinger Press, 2002.

ON THE INTERNET

Blended Family Association of America
www.usabfa.org

Bonus Families
www.bonusfamilies.com

Living With Stepparents
kidshealth.org/kid/feeling/home_family/blended.html

National Stepfamily Resource Center
www.stepfamily.info

Step Parenting Tips
www.blended-families.com

The Stepfamily Foundation
www.stepfamily.org

Bibliography

Davis. Kimberly. "Making Blended Families Work." *Ebony*, October 2000.

Cincinnati Children's Hospital. Advice for Parents, www.cincinnatichildrens.org/health/yh/archives/2005/spring/blended-family.htm.

Hetherington, E. Mavis. *For Better or Worse, Divorce Reconsidered.* New York: Hyperion, 2001.

Lambert, Andrea. "Perceptions of Romantic Relationships in Adult Children of Divorce." Paper presented at the annual meeting of the International Communication Association, TBA, San Francisco, CA, May 23, 2007, http://www.allacademic.com/meta/p171110_index.html.

Marquardt, Elizabeth. *Between Two Worlds: The Inner Lives of Children of Divorce.* New York: Three Rivers Press, 2006.

Thurman, Paul. "One Stepfather's Advice," ezinearticles.com/?One-Stepfathers-Advice&id=2136122.

Wallerstein, Judith. *The Unexpected Legacy of Divorce: A 25-Year Landmark Study.* New York: Hyperion, 2000.

Index

America 10, 21

baby 43

change 18, 26, 31, 43, 52, 60
church 56
college 50
contention 28, 38
control 8, 17

discipline 17, 36, 37, 39, 44
divorce 10, 12, 13, 19, 29, 41

family
    extended 23
    nuclear 9, 10

gender roles 9

jealousy 15, 31, 34, 42

parents
    biological 10, 17, 18, 20–23, 54, 55
    father 23, 24, 47–50, 54

grandparents 23, 28, 31, 32, 34
mother 10, 28–31, 34, 39, 43, 52, 53
single 10, 11, 17, 53, 57
stepfather 10, 23, 24, 27, 47–50, 53
stepmother 8, 10, 23, 28, 31, 35
permission 22, 52, 53

remarriage 13, 17
research 10, 12, 13, 25, 26
respect 27, 39

school 17, 24, 26, 27, 30, 31, 50, 56
security 9
separation 22
sibling
    brother 34, 53
    sister 41, 53
    step 10, 15, 26, 55
stress 10, 12, 15, 16, 18, 36

teenage 21, 53
tradition 9, 10, 17, 22, 56, 58

wedding 22, 43, 56, 58, 59
week 9, 28, 39, 41
weekend 28, 31, 34, 50

vacation 30–32, 46

About the Author and the Consultant

AUTHOR

Rae Simons came from a family of five children, and she now has three children of her own. Her role in her "nuclear" family as well as in her extended family continues to shape her life in many ways. As a middle school teacher, she worked closely with a wide range of family configurations. She has written many educational books for young adults.

CONSULTANT

Gallup has studied human nature and behavior for more than seventy years. Gallup's reputation for delivering relevant, timely, and visionary research on what people around the world think and feel is the cornerstone of the organization. Gallup employs many of the world's leading scientists in management, economics, psychology, and sociology, and its consultants assist leaders in identifying and monitoring behavioral economic indicators worldwide. Gallup consultants help organizations boost organic growth by increasing customer engagement and maximizing employee productivity through measurement tools, coursework, and strategic advisory services. Gallup's 2,000 professionals deliver services at client organizations, through the Web, at Gallup University's campuses, and in forty offices around the world.